SIGNIFICANT CHURCH HISTORY

SIGNIFICANT
CHURCH HISTORY

by

R. GORDON MILBURN

JAMES CLARKE & CO. LIMITED
33 STORE STREET,
LONDON, W.C.1.

First published 1959

To
H. H. PRICE
in gratitude and affection

Printed in Great Britain by
The Camelot Press Ltd., London and Southampton

CONTENTS

		PAGE
	Preface	7
I	Historical Significance	9
II	The Fact of Change	16
III	Reductive Reinterpretation	24
IV	The Long Drift	28
V	The Alternative Road	44
	Appendix	69
	Some Suggestions	72

PREFACE

I IMAGINE (publishers will know whether I am right) that since the First World War there must, at any time, have been hundreds of persons of but very limited abilities endeavouring to write books, not because we had literary ambitions or liked writing (it has, in fact, been very wearisome), but because it felt as though the situation were calling upon us to do our best to contribute to the re-laying of the moral and spiritual foundations of modern life. One never knows what commonplace motives may not lie behind one's best endeavours, but so far as consciousness goes we have simply wanted so to write that our readers would think and feel about the things that matter better than they would have thought and felt had they never read us.

A combination of interests has, however, hitherto made the publication of such books as this (as well as other means of expression) impracticable.

R. GORDON MILBURN.

CHESHAM BOIS.
May, 1959.

I

HISTORICAL SIGNIFICANCE

IN these pages we shall be considering the successive phases of the impact of modern thought upon the Church of England during the last hundred, and more especially during the last forty, years and the changing reactions of the Church thereto. We shall not be concerned with opinion outside the Christian Church. It is of the curve of changing thought within our own Church that we shall be thinking. The faith of a Church is rather like some heavenly body, the path of which can be inferred by observing its position on a number of successive occasions, and in the Church of England four successive phases of its reaction to the increasing hold of scientific thinking over the human mind can be clearly distinguished. We wonder what they imply as indications of the truth or falsity of religion. We shall not be discussing this question directly, for this is a historical, not a metaphysical essay, but if the story is properly told a good deal of its significance will become apparent. Our aim will not be to gather or impart information but to get known facts into a perspective which will prove revealing. In past ages this fundamental issue as to the truth of religion in general was obscured by the interest of Church historians in minor differences, such as that between Catholic and Protestant, the general validity of a religious outlook being taken for granted. During the last hundred years, however, questions of a more basic and universal character have increasingly made themselves felt. They impart a deep significance to all events bearing upon them.

Strictly speaking, it is rather loose language to talk about the truth of religion, because religion is not a system of ideas, as the word "truth" naturally suggests, but an attitude of a person's whole self different in kind from any purely secular one. But the expression is commonly used and need not be ambiguous. To put it rather more concretely: There is a spirit in the hymns of the nineteenth century which mark our starting-point. Religion is that spirit. It has been the *raison d'être* of the whole Christian Church until now. It has been nourished by beliefs largely legendary, largely purely speculative. Scientific habits of thought are undermining it, but it is not yet clear to any impartial observer whether it is nevertheless linked with a truth beyond all science or whether, for lack of such, it is destined to extinction in Western civilization. This constant background issue dwarfs all details and constitutes the main ground of their significance.

A second ground of significance is the Church's ability or inability to react to new situations creatively with acts of clear-eyed choice, to grasp novel positions and to perceive new possibilities. An event, or simple non-occurrence of any event, which indicates that ability or inability is historically significant, however unimportant it may be in itself. A feeble Report of some commission of inquiry for example.

Four impulsions may push a Church passively along. One is prescribed order and routine. The second is

practical considerations. The third is principles un-
thinkingly applied, with a staunch loyalty to one's own
opinions that is unconsciously egoistic. The fourth is
the trend of the times. A school of thought may have
become fashionable and a Church may accommodate
itself to new tendencies as inertly as it may adhere to
old ones. And so one must observe little things and
consider how a Church's behaviour represents real
vital responses, how far the helpless drifting of a storm-
tossed wreck. Indications therefore on a Church's
part of inability to react creatively to cultural change
should be noted, for they raise the question of how
much they are symptomatic.

Every period of history has had its unseen alternative in a better might-have-been. At any given point
of history there is some trend of events in actual
process, but also the possibility of another and better
line of development if certain difficult, but not impossible, moral conditions are fulfilled. Events are
the consequences of rejections of alternatives in the
past, and very often they bear the character of a
nemesis. They stand as an endless line of tombstones
to things that might have been but never were. Often
they mark the graves of glories we had not big enough
souls to achieve. The chief lessons of history are to be
learnt from events that never happened. If, then, a
Church is indeed an institution for the realization,
through right relationship with an Unseen, of a kind
of life, personal and collective, higher than would
otherwise have been possible we may view the
tragedies of history as partly due to the moral failures
of Churches which had forgotten that they had duties
to humanity and civilization wider than those

which (quite rightly) constitute their primary interest.

These considerations apply alike to the moral and to the intellectual occasions with which a Church from time to time is faced. In both cases there is the need for alertness of spirit and the danger of an unthinking compliance with the customary. A Church, then, being a society for helping men to live a higher kind of life, to think truer thoughts, and to have deeper inward experiences, than would be possible for them without religion, any given period of a Church's history can be regarded as the story of the moral occasions through which it had to make good the supernatural element given to it to vindicate on pain of sinning against the Spirit.

Of more specifically moral rather than intellectual occasions one example must suffice. In the days when the British *raj* in India seemed secure the attitude of the bulk of those white men who professed Christianity toward Indians as such was incompatible with Christian principles. It would be unjust to equate that attitude with that of white South Africa to black. But, by and large, the Christian Church in India did fail to make good its own Christianity in matters of social and racial ethics. At the time of the Ilbert Bill agitation in 1884 English politics and English Christianity stood where the road divided. Both took the road of master-race imperialism. He who says A must say B, and the course we then entered upon led by its inherent logic to the Rowlatt Act and to the massacre of Amritsar. I have referred to these events chiefly in order to emphasize the fact that the life of a Church consists of meeting an endless series of moral and intellectual challenges, traditional doctrine and routine procedure being more of the nature of connecting threads between occasion and occasion than the substance of which a living Church can be composed.

Only history can bring this perspective home to our consciences, only history can reveal the ever-changing soul of the Church as it was yesterday in this place and in that the day before. And history can do so only when the historian has a true sense for the relative significance of events. There are different levels of significance for the Church historian. The deepest, as we have seen, is that which springs directly from the permanent, basic issue between a religious and a non-religious world-view as a matter of metaphysical truth. There is very little metaphysical significance in the difference between orthodoxy and heresy or between one Christian body and another in comparison with the fundamental difference between a religious and a non-religious outlook on existence. Religion is the response of man to the Supernatural in faith that the Supernatural will, because of its utter goodness, respond to him. Over against this faith stands the postulate of positivism that there is no Supernatural, no God, no unseen love-object to which a man can be related through prayer and meditation, no experience of redemption, at-one-ment, or grace, no souls of the departed, no future realization of the latent powers merely hinted at in man's earthly life. Where lies the truth? The main interest in the story of any uncompleted exploration must lie in the point already reached. The present state of inquiry into the possibility of an extension of consciousness beyond the phenomenal world must overshadow all interest in events as such, and especially those of long ago.

There is therefore a vast existential difference between contemporary history and the chronicles of past ages. It is the difference between living and dead history. There is nothing vital in the fact that once upon a time there was one theologian who held one opinion and another who held another and that some synod decided in favour of this view or that. It does not follow that because some event had important consequences it is therefore important for us to have a knowledge of it. On the contrary, it is arguable that a sense of the importance of the religious controversies of long ago is positively injurious to the average clergyman since it may very well give him a very artificial scale of values and deaden his power of response to present conditions. The more important we feel an ancient issue to have been the more likely shall we be to think in terms of it, and the less capable of seeing the real issues at stake in the life of humanity around us. A theology based upon a traditional body of doctrines must tend to make the doctrines and practices themselves the object of religious devotion. Originally a means to something beyond themselves, they tend to become ends in themselves, and a study of the ancient controversies through which those doctrines were fashioned inevitably tends to treat them as the important things.

There is something about this antiquarian type of religion which puts it out of right relationship with the real world and impedes its proper functioning. It is as though we had been deported to a land beyond the seas, leaving our temples behind us. Antiquarian theology is a sort of ferry service for taking passengers back for Sunday services. But the gulf between the old land and the new is becoming wider every year and those who cross it fewer.

The significance of the past is thus derived from the deep anxieties of the present day. They are partly moral, partly intellectual, but above all there is anxiety as to whether a new synthesis of faith and truth is really possible, and, if so, on what lines it will have to be. A history of modern religious thought must reflect these uncertainties and anxieties; otherwise it would misrepresent the inward character of the situation.

II

THE FACT OF CHANGE

THROUGHOUT the last hundred years Christian doctrine has been in process of continuous change. Since this is a fact, but since it is also a fact that the dogma of an immutable and infallible creed is still nominally maintained, organized religion is now in danger of degenerating into a loose system of make-believe for parochial purposes. This may not be the best possible way of putting it, but something of the sort should be pictured as the general background of the period. The main cause at work to produce this result has already been indicated—namely, the permeation of all civilization with a spirit which begins with science and ends with positivism, and whatever positivism may lead to.

A hundred years ago is a very good point for the Church history of modern times to start from because we thus get two strongly marked phases of the Christian religion standing in the sharpest of possible contrasts with one another, and between them, if we may avail ourselves of a little schematism, two intermediate phases. It is not necessary to discuss the assumptions of Christian faith prior to 1860. The general type of religion in this country during the eighteen fifties is well known. (I have sketched a brief outline of it elsewhere.) One point, however, may be noted. A religious man might be a scientist because science meant for him, not a world-view or way of thinking inimical to religion, but an exact and extensive knowledge of the wonderful works of God. Revelation meant divinely imparted information and comprised everything in the Bible, which was, in effect, a reserved area to which the ordinary uniformities of nature did not necessarily apply. Like all our other interests and experiences, science might, indeed, be an occasion for a religious mood, but it was something outside religion—not an element in it or a limiting condition which could determine its scope. Religion was an autonomous attitude of the soul and the creed in which it found expression was independent of all other considerations, such as scientific opinion.

But this is not what science, as a motive force in the history of religion, means. If by "science" we merely mean the conclusions reached by the natural sciences, it is something which has very little to do with modern religion. All the churches accept those conclusions with regard to things in general. All that they have had to do is slightly to modify their reserved area. But science, in the sense relevant to current Church history, is much more than this. It is an intellectual passion which seizes upon any subject-matter offered to it, analyses it, tears it to pieces, and reconstitutes it as a web of causal connections. The great mutation of Anglican religion which may be dated as having begun in the year 1860, consisted of the taking of this intellectual hunger into itself. By far the greater part of this mentality which has entered into the Christian ministry has probably come in by the Church's own door of biblical theology, the most revolutionary of all the sciences.

B

Of course, there were fundamentalists who protested, but what a serious student has to fasten his attention upon is, not a few splash incidents which make copy for journalists, but general trends and what they point to. Still more keenly will he observe any wave of genuinely creative life which may have passed. The first half of this period of spiritual change may be regarded, perhaps, as representing little more than a relaxed hold of the Old Christianity over the mind of the age, due directly to the influence of science of all kinds. In view of the strong Latitudinarian element in the Anglican tradition, this relaxation of the Old faith is not strange, but the Neo-Tractarian reformation at the end of the century deserves closer study because, within the limits of the Church, it did, both intellectually and in other ways, achieve a great deal. And yet it somehow gives one the strong impression that, for one's soul's health, one must seek for truth and be deluded, for reality and find a myth.

Its leading feature was the unreserved acceptance, in general principle, of both biblical criticism and natural science, combined with a definite creed held to in faith. This was a possible attitude for the Neo-Tractarian leaders because they were firmly, though mistakenly, convinced that rigorous critical methods would establish their doctrinal position. A critically examined New Testament thus took the place of an uncriticizable Bible. Religion thereby acquired a dual character; on the one hand there was faith; on the other there was a secular culture welcomed as a work of the Holy Spirit. When the idea of the Spirit is the dominant factor in one's total outlook nature, science, literature, all become transfigured. There is a very beautiful passage to this effect in Gore's *Bampton Lectures*, p. 138. And if religion can thus welcome science, there is no reason, it was felt, why science should not welcome religion. It seemed, in 1890, as though the new orthodoxy were having the best of both worlds.

This period ended in the spring of 1914 with an incident which was logically tantamount to a collapse of the foundations of the new orthodoxy. A semi-public controversy between the Regius Professor of Divinity at Oxford, Dr. William Sanday, and the Rev. J. M. Thompson, a modernist don of Magdalen College, on the subject of the historicity of the Virgin Birth resulted in the confession of the orthodox champion that he had come to the conclusion that he had been mistaken and that the doctrine in question was critically untenable. And when at length, about twenty years later, the Archbishop's Committee on Doctrine issued its Report, it acknowledged the possibility that a clergyman might abandon belief in the Virgin Birth without thereby showing himself unfit for his office. There are, of course, other articles of the Creeds which are disputed within the borders of the Church, but as a matter of historical fact it was on the question of the Virgin Birth that the principle of acceptance of the creeds as a rule of faith broke down.

Is this expression warranted? Let us consider. Neo-Tractarian orthodoxy was a rule of faith, it is true, but only in a secondary way. It depended upon the prior discovery of the critical, but open-minded, reason that the New Testament writers were so reliable as to be virtually infallible. The further discovery of a six-century-long divine guidance of the Church's thought itself presupposed that activity of the open-minded critical reason. The Church's rule of faith should therefore have been regarded as being, in principle, open to critical re-examination whenever the requisite and intellectual conditions were forthcoming. This was the principle which had justified the revolt of the Neo-Tractarians themselves against the old fundamental-ism. In the instance just quoted there are no more grounds for impugning the moral and intellectual qualifications of Professor Sanday and Mr. Thompson than there are for questioning those of the reformers twenty-five years earlier. An occasion for the applica-tion of the principle of open-minded biblical criticism had arisen, and the evidence against the truth of the challenged doctrine (quite apart from all question of miracles) was overwhelming. What would have been the ideal reaction of the Church to such a situation had not a world war broken out just at that moment?

The purpose of this essay is not to retail information about events, but to help the reader to reflect upon them, the first thing to do on such an occasion being to suspend judgement until all the relevant factors in the case have been reviewed.

The first factor to be considered is the principle of open-minded historical criticism. It is the rule that the conclusions of biblical criticism must be deter-mined by the evidence only, whether it point to supernatural influences at work or not. Genuine his-torical inquiry must not allow itself to be overruled by postulates of any kind, whether it be in the form of a rule of faith or in that of the exclusion of the miracu-lous. Both sorts of postulates are ways of begging the question when the supernatural itself is the subject of inquiry.

The second factor in the case is the fact that the principle of open-mindedness had been implicit in the Anglicanism of the 'eighties and 'nineties, and it was in this sign that the Neo-Tractarian leaders had won their victory over fundamentalism. They had been confident that they were standing for a many-sided truth in its wholeness; they were "concerned to be rational"; they proclaimed the principle of "In the light, though it be but to perish". Ought not, then, the principle in question to be held as a definite dogma of Anglicanism in the light of which all older principles ought to be reviewed?

There is another aspect of the case. A people which loses a faith or a myth needs, for its soul's health, some compensating value, and this, in the long run, can be gained only through some new mythology, whether it be of a sacred or of a secular character. Instances of secular mythologies will readily suggest themselves.

Our second period thus ended in questions never expressly asked, problems that never emerged into clear consciousness. But if the reader will think it all over he will see that they were there and that they went much farther than doubts about the truth of a legend.

A critical discussion of the Virgin Birth would not fall within the scope of this essay. Since, however, the reader may not be familiar with the subject, I will mention just one or two points. The story appears for the first time at least ninety years after the event, the Annunciation, if a fact, being reckoned as having

taken place in 7 B.C., the Birth stories as about A.D. 85,
though perhaps a few years earlier. That of itself
would ordinarily be enough to make a psychical
researcher dismiss a story of similar kind without
further investigation. The evidence of the intervening
period, which is fairly definite and of various kinds, is
against the truth of the story. The circumstances were
such as to suggest the idea, even if it had no basis in
fact, so that the occurrence of that idea in St. Matthew
and St. Luke does not necessarily point to more than
the prevalence of it toward the end of the first century.
There are arguments from the text of the Birth
narratives themselves and from certain manuscript
readings. But the simplest procedure is to read the
Gospel stories themselves with the question in mind:
Is this fact or legend? If one's first impression is that
we are in the realm of imaginative ideas throughout,
one must ask what corroborative evidence there is to
show that one is wrong after all. There is no corroborative evidence, unless one chooses so to regard a
Jewish scandal story of later origin, clearly concocted
as a reply to the idea of the Virgin Birth.

A simple following of the course of events has
brought us to a point at which we had to pause and
reflect. When we did so we saw that a certain challenge
to traditional doctrine was only too well founded and
that it moreover involved the breakdown of the
guiding principles of the dominant school of orthodoxy
which held the two creeds of the undivided Church
to be sacrosanct. It is not a matter to be dismissed
as a passing incident. The proven untenability of a
dogma held at the same time to be inviolable surely

requires something more than a tolerated division of opinion. In the present case there is an alternative. Legends still current and venerated, yet treated symbolically and not as history, may sometimes prove a better medium of meditation than stories accepted as literal fact. Many might well be taken in sermons as symbols of that attitude of submissive receptivity whereby the soul receives God into itself. There is ample enough precedent for the metaphorical treatment to history to enable such a procedure to pass muster as good Catholicism. It would have been a small matter in comparison with the enormous change in the Church's doctrinal outlook which marks the difference between the first and second periods within the last hundred years. Incidents of this kind, however, mark the breakdown of a ground of faith. In the first period of modern Church history faith rested on an infallible book, in the second upon the theory of a divine guidance of the Church which guaranteed the truth of its formal creed. Since 1914 the Church itself has been increasingly uncertain as to what really is the true basis of religious belief.

III

REDUCTIVE REINTERPRETATION

THE various successive phases of modern religion of course, overlap, just as the Stone, Bronze, and Iron Ages overlapped, and yet the features of each religious period stand out fairly distinctly. At the present moment (May, 1959) we stand on the threshold of the fourth epoch, which is, indeed, in its first beginnings already here. It is the third age culture to which the bulk of us belong, but it is the fourth phase of modern religion which reveals to us, as it were in an apocalypse, the end to which our ways of life and thought are leading us, and so it will be instructive to take a glance at the coming age before we examine our own.

Its salient characteristic is the penetration of the churches by those radical denials which constitute the mark of a secularist, as opposed to a religious, world-view. There are Christian ministers and theologians who are abandoning belief in a personal God, in the operation of the Holy Spirit, in the Incarnation, in a future life, and in all other Christian doctrines as formerly held, but without saying so in so many words. One often has to discover this negative trend of a writer's thought by comparing one passage with another, noting significant silences, and reading between the lines. This is especially noticeable in the case with regard to disbelief in any life after death, a disbelief most clearly noticeable in the writings of

Neo-Lutherans in Germany and America, but also observable in other most unlikely quarters. In the *New Outline of Modern Knowledge* the subject of survival does not seem to be discussed at all—not even in the articles on Psychical Research, Theism, or Metaphysical Speculation, and Professor Zaehner's article, which reads like a manifesto in favour of Roman Catholicism, apparently identifies eternal life with Jung's collective unconscious. Neither Jesus Christ nor anyone else has ever, according to these theologians, survived bodily death or existed before he was born.

The means by which this secularization of religious thought is effected is what is called "reinterpretation". This means assigning new, secular meanings to the traditional language of religion. It is usually done by bringing some idea derived from general culture (in most cases from Freud or Jung) into connection with some religious term, but definitions are avoided and how much of the traditional meaning of it is being dropped is not stated, and so we are left with a blurr of overtones, religious, ethical, and psychological, which sound profound but convey no definite meaning. "Reinterpretation" is not a new word. It has been used by orthodox writers to denote the employment of modern locutions in place of manners of speech no longer in common usage. In the mouth of positivists it indicates a procedure which might be called Reductive Theology—that is to say, the reduction of a religious to a secular meaning of words by means of equivocal language.

'Reinterpretation' has entered into modern theology as the name for the methods of the Neo-Lutheran school of demythologizers. In this case I do not suggest that there has been the least bit of guileful intention. The leading exponent of this line of thought, Professor Bultmann, has made it quite clear that, in his view, doctrines unacceptable to biologically-minded people should be rejected as mythological except in so far as they can be thus reinterpreted. His main contention, to the effect that Lutheran formulas can be reinterpreted in the light of Heidegger's philosophy, is too remote from anything of much interest to ourselves to call for further discussion. I have every respect for Professor Bultmann and I greatly admire the thoroughness of German theology, but such reinterpretation as this would not merely be valueless on this side of the Channel; it would be morally dangerous. One has but to imagine this sort of equivocation in common parochial practice to feel its objectionableness. At Eastertide 1957 I listened to a sermon on the Resurrection by a clergyman regarded as orthodox. His language was equally compatible with belief and with disbelief in personal survival. I mentioned the case to another clergyman and said that I had half a mind to write and ask the preacher what he meant to imply. The other clergyman replied, "He would certainly say that he did believe in survival, whatever he thought in his heart of hearts." Would that there might be carven on every pulpit in our country these words of Achilles:

> That man is hateful as the gates of death
> Who thinketh one thing and another saith.

Reductive theology can be of no value whatever to unbelievers of all sorts because they already possess the substance of it in secular language, which is much more suitable. Christian phrases to express our ordinary thoughts is but rigmarole at best; introduced into public worship it is a great deal worse.

Secret unbelief veiled in the language of faith appears to be the goal toward which the Church of Christ is drifting. For, once more, it is not the abandonment of religion and the choice of rationalism in its place that we now observe, but the direction in which Christian thought is being driven—namely, to something very like verbal fraud. If a preacher is once suspected of reinterpretation one listens suspiciously for double meanings, not trustfully, for edification. Every sermon preached now requires a glossary of terms, for all have become ambiguous. When, for instance, Professor Bultmann speaks of Christ as God's eschatological emissary in bringing a redemption which is not a supernatural but a historical event, what he seems to mean is that Christ was the figure thrown up by the forces of evolution, the impression made by whose death generated an effectual ethic of detachment otherwise impossible. He may mean more than this or he may not. He is, of course, quite sincere. Positivist writers in such journals as the *Hibbert* employ still more deceptive language. A habit of changing the meaning of words to suit a writer's or preacher's personal philosophy is seeping into the Church as a sort of mock orthodoxy, and it is for the Church to consider how far it is itself responsible for it through its own mental inertia, its own failure to find a creative response to the challenge of the situation.

IV

THE LONG DRIFT

THE third phase of modern religion is that which is leading to the fourth. That is by far the most significant aspect of it and therefore, in a study of perspective such as this essay, we must concentrate our attention upon it. Our aim must be to become more clearly conscious of those features of our present-day religion in virtue of which it is leading to the fourth stage, already described. No accusations need be levelled. If, whether we follow a more liberal or a more conservative path, the death of faith is inevitable no one can be blamed for not keeping it alive. But we may observe more closely how it is all happening, and we may still hope that faith may live.

The third epoch—the period of the forty years' drift —may roughly be dated from 1914 to the time when the influence of demythologizing Lutheranism began to make itself felt. *Kerygma and Myth* was published in 1954. When I speak of this period as one of drift I am referring to its intellectual aspect only, for, before all things, it was a time marked by failure to foresee and prepare for what was coming. One gets the impression of a myopic, hand-to-mouth opportunism, with no sense for anything that lies beyond the routine of the moment, no comprehensive vision, no initiative on the part of those who ought to have been our local intellectual leaders, no prophetic courage, no vital contact between the universities and the parishes. Not that good work is not being done on the basis of things as they were fifty years ago. Most certainly there is, but it now rests on presuppositions which history has already invalidated, so that individual excellence may at times seem to be shrouded in collective unreality.

The most prominent feature of today's religion is the tendency for means to inhibit ends. In order that church services may be popularized, the deeper and harder elements in religion are set aside. Go into a place of worship on one of the major festivals or commemorations of the Church: in a very large number of cases you will find thought watered down, conviction unfelt, dry subjects avoided. The managerial standpoint, concerned with the successful running of Church institutions, is taking the place of that of the prophet, the seer, the philosopher, and the evangelist. The big ideas round which religion used to revolve are losing their urgency. Religion is in a state of inward decay. There is less substance in it, less vital responsiveness. I am not referring to sacramental worship or teaching which, though narrowly circumscribed, is still alive, but to a general fading out of the other world, which is therefore dropped as not being what people want. In its place there comes the brief, bright, pleasant chat, or at least a well-meant effort in that direction. When the main object of a parish is to keep an interest in church services alive, attractions must come first and means take precedence of ends. Popularization is in principle secularization and is therefore likely to lead on to the fourth phase of modern religion on its less intellectual side.

It is indeed true that if there is no longer any desire for peace with God, for a new heart, for a higher life hereafter for which we must prepare now, for daily grace received through prayer, and at last the beatific vision and union with God, there is much to be said for a well-considered plan for second-bests. But the Church's second-bests are rarely big and heavy enough. It never thinks of wondering what serious interests it should offer to those who do not want personal religion but might well respond to subjects bearing on Christian social ethics or even to speculative metaphysics relevant to a spiritual world-view. If practical objections to such a course are too strong the fact does but illustrate the supremacy of the managerial standpoint in the Church—a supremacy based upon short-term opportunist considerations. I am not, at this point, arguing what ought, or ought not, to be, but endeavouring to sketch the nature of the phases through which religion in the Church of England is passing. We have noticed that a general weakening of the religious consciousness throughout English Christendom is transforming local churches into centres for keeping congregations together as an end in itself independently of any genuinely religious motive. The veiled secularism of the fourth stage of organized religion in modern times is the next station ahead of us if this line of slow, inward disintegration continues. For perhaps the most significant thing about popular religion is the absence of any operative supernaturalism in it. Miracles come in occasionally, of course, but only as Bible stories; there is little or nothing in it about any sort of personal relationship with a Beyond. One does not talk about sin and redemption at pleasant Sunday tea-parties. From a purely practical point of view there may be much to be said for light programme religion. But from the point of view of historical studies which have to trace the latent significance of the course of events immediate values are not the main point. Having already seen where, in the absence of much painful reflection, the trend of things is taking us, we have to consider the relation of this type of religion to that trend. If, in the case of any given parish whatever, we accept the sufficiency of it, are we not thereby contributing to the coming of what it tends to result in?

There is something ominous about the whole ecclesiastical scene. For either Fate is in the very act of tearing to shreds the illusions which, for nineteen centuries, brought us the bread of life, or the pearl of great price, although a real possibility, is likely to be lost to us for a thousand years owing to our failure to find the right response to the present situation. Whichever way we look at it, it is our present habits of thought and practice which are carrying us along to the next stage ahead, and if that stage is a state of hollow make-believe it will be our present habits of thought which will be responsible. We need a psychoanalysis, not of anything so intellectually elusive as the spirit of religion, but of the tastes, tempers, and tendencies commonly associated with it. For religion is rarely met with except in combination with an alloy. Let us suspect our good motives; we do not know what may not be lurking behind them. Our reasons for running our parishes as we do and for preaching as we do may be well enough up to a point, but there is something wrong with us nevertheless.

One very favourite plea for disregard of the fundamental issue between faith and modern philosophy is
that a preacher should always have primary regard
for the simple souls of his congregation. Not that he
should want to educate them, but that he should
shield them from every breath of doubt. This principle
readily slides into the absurd assumption that all the
members of any given congregation are simple souls.
I once asked the chaplain of Shillong, the summer seat
of the Government of Eastern Bengal, whether he did
not find it very difficult to prepare sermons for such
brainy people as the members of the various Government secretariats. He replied, "I find that they need
very simple teaching." He would have found the same
in the case of a congregation composed of Bertrand
Russells. Even in those cases in which a clergyman has
knowledge enough for the most up-to-date of dis-
courses, he will talk on fundamentalist lines "lest",
as one such responsible cleric put it to me, "one cause
one of these little ones to stumble". The stumbling in
question did not mean mortal sin, but consideration
of a well-known point of New Testament criticism, and
the little ones on this particular occasion were under-
graduates and, perhaps, college dons.

On another occasion I had written an Eastertide
sermon for a clergyman who wanted me to preach for
him. I told him that it was based on St. Paul's list of
Appearances and that it interpreted the Resurrection
as a case of telepathy from the dead. It assumed that a
living Christ was manifesting himself in that way
from another plane of existence. He would not allow
me to preach it. I showed it to another clergyman,
who did not think it bad, but did not want me to let

his wife see it. She is a thoughtful, educated woman, interested in what little she knows about critical studies, and the mother of intelligent children who may soon be asking her questions. There did not seem to be any conscious desire on his part to keep her in the dark; it was just clerical instinct.

There certainly is the fact that to meet the intellectual requirements of the situation as they ought to be met, even in country parishes, would require a knowledge and ability far beyond one's own. When once this obvious fact is recognized, diocesan problems arise; various means for meeting the difficulty can be imagined. But a sense of the gravity of the problem and of one's own inadequacy must come first.

Simple souls, in the sense required by the preacher who has nothing but the very simplest of foodstuffs to offer, are rapidly becoming extinct. Talk to your domestic helper, or read Rowntree and Layers' *English Life and Leisure*. It is not only jaded intellectuals who look upon religion as "kid's stuff". Souls are not naturally so simple or so pained by unorthodoxy. It is difficult to express oneself with reverence for all sincere faith and devotion and yet to show that these may degenerate into fixations which are blinding us to the more fundamental problems of faith and truth. Can it even be, sometimes, that we clergy do not want to understand—do not want to know that people can go to church hungry for intellectual help, not against doubt in the abstract, but with regard to some particular source of doubt; that when they come their heart sinketh within them at the seeming crudity, childishness, or irrelevance of what they hear, and that one day this happens for the last time?

C

The difficulty here from a manager's point of view is that to deal with points of criticism in church would be to put doubts into the heads of people who had never entertained them before. But in the first place, this is untruthful. If you know that there are valid grounds for questioning the truth of some biblical story, why should your religion prompt you to conceal the fact? Why should a truthful man wish that the faith of other people should be too crude to be true, too open to criticism to be secure? As mere educational tactics, people should learn the principles of biblical criticism from the Church first; it draws half of the enemy's teeth. But that is putting it on too low a ground. Let us be truthful because we pray, "Increase in us *true* religion"—the religion of truth—"that all we who profess and call ourselves Christians may be led into the way of truth and magnify thy holy name *worthily*"—without any abandonment of the highest standards, intellectual or other. The ideal concepts of the Church seem to be at variance with parochial practice today, or at least are not effectively operative.

Things come about in strange ways. We have been tracing the curve of history drawn by the influence of scientific habits of thought upon religion. We distinguished four phases. In the first period religion was uninfluenced by science; the two belonged to different departments of the mind. But religion was very zealous for truth as it understood it. The second phase came as a creative synthesis of faith, science, and illusion. Assured of truth, the Church welcomed science without realizing the difference between the objective conclusions of the particular sciences, on the one hand, and the analytic, disintegrative temper of science on the other. By making its revolutionary response to the challenge of objective science it found itself faced with the deeper, subjective challenge of the scientific spirit. The helplessness of the Church in the presence of this inward problem, of which it is not more than half aware, goes a good way toward explaining the weaknesses it has displayed throughout the third period of modern Church history. With the maggot of modern-mindedness gnawing, unknown, at his own faith, how can a parish priest call on his unbelieving parishioners for serious talks about things that matter? He can still be a social manager, but not a prophet or a guide for troubled souls.

It may be objected that this is palpably untrue of the Anglo-Catholic clergy. They seem to possess an abundance of far from modern beliefs. This may be true, but it does not go very far toward effecting a synthesis of faith and truth or toward laying afresh the spiritual foundations of our national life. These are the big things; beliefs call for analysis before we can assess their value. Faith is a very complex thing and can be of very varied nature (even when belief is the same) according to the proportions in which the various elements in it are mixed together. One element often found in it is what might be called addiction. People may have so highly developed a taste for ideas of some particular kind that they cannot give them up. It is not exactly compulsive thinking, but an appetite over which rational thought may exercise as little influence as over cigarette-smoking. Addiction is by no means peculiar to religion; the mechanist theory of science was once very often a matter of addiction.

But it is Anglo-Catholicism which most clearly raises the question of the relation of addiction to religion. An extreme instance will illustrate the point best. Not very long ago I heard a preacher—a most excellent person—declare that Mary was the most perfect human being, apart from Christ himself, who had ever lived. He could not possibly know that there are not ten thousand better women alive in England today. When he venerates the Blessed Sacrament, he declares, "Blessed be the great Mother of God, Mary most holy!" In order to keep such a hot-house plant alive, a devotee must shut and lock the door of his mind against any line of study which might spoil this idealized mental picture, for an addiction as such is out of all relationship to rational thought of any kind, and it will defend itself, if attacked, as though it were an independent entity. All emotionally held ideas, but especially any idea of the Divine concrete enough to be adored or venerated, such as Christ or some heathen deity, is, subjectively viewed, primarily of the nature of, or akin to, an addiction. Yet it may nevertheless quite conceivably, in certain combinations, be an organ of truth. To pass as that, however, it must be tested by whatever criteria we may possess, with absolute honesty.

We have come to a point at which it is terribly difficult to say what ought to be said without saying it in such a way that it were better left unsaid. Consider: It is immeasurably more important that those who proclaim a higher truth than secular thought has discovered should both be absolutely straightforward and should give the impression of absolute straightforwardness than that any particular opinion should

prevail. There is a vast amount of unstraightforward-
ness in the Church, but it is so unconscious that those
most concerned are quite unaware that their conduct
is unstraightforward. If an outsider mentions it, it is
discounted as an attack on religion, and no one of
authority and influence in the Church will call a
spade a spade.

Consider, first, whether it is morally right that we
should wilfully mislead those who trust us or deliber-
ately leave them in the dark on the plea that they are
simple souls? Think how many unworthy motives may
lurk behind this misplaced tenderness. Is there not
something wilfully untruthful about it, whatever its
motives?

Consider next whether there does not prevail in the
Church today an attitude of acquiescence in things as
we find them that is incompatible with zeal either for
truth or for righteousness. So far as we are concerned
for such things it is as citizens or individuals—not as
Christians. Examples would be too contentious for the
present context and, of course, there are individual
Christians of whom this generalization does not hold
good. But, broadly speaking, it is no part of our
religion to fling fire upon the earth.

Consider yet again. There is at the present moment
an actual conflict within the soul of the Church
between devotion and truth which the Christian conscience does not know how to reconcile. When conclusions as to historical fact are derived from addictions
fostered out of all relationship to rational thought,
special pleading is a form of untruthfulness. When
one finds defenders of orthodoxy palpably ignoring
the weight of evidence and arguing instead from what

God could do if he chose, and urging that since such and such an occasion made it appropriate for him to stage (a disgusting word, but it is what the apologist really means) a series of portents (if, as must doubtless have been the case, his feelings coincided with those of the theologians in question), he therefore did produce them—when one reads such arguments one feels in despair. One could go on exposing the absurd irrelevancy of premises to conclusion in such arguments and the reckless way in which they would raise insoluble difficulties if one took them seriously. But all derision is of the devil, and in matters of religion doubly and trebly so, and the point need not be further pursued. Unscrupulous apologetics is but one instance of a lowered ethical content in our religion and more especially of our diminished sense of truth.

Our picture of the third phase of modern religion is that of a drifting Church trying to make an outward conservatism a substitute for a fading faith. And as genuine conviction declines the moral inspiration it possessed declines with it. The main cause of this decline has been sufficiently noted; it is the influence of the scientific temper beyond the borders of strict science. The Church is now like a caterpillar in which an ichneumon fly has laid its eggs. Its ministers may be socially active and useful, but their inward parts—their faith, their hope, their vision—are being eaten away.

Of more definitely moral causes which affect the Church collectively, as elements in its corporate outlook and traditions, self-interest and self-centredness are the most in evidence. When a parish priest neglects his non-churchgoing parishioners he represents the self-interested Church concerned only with getting members for itself, not with the disinterested service of man or of the nation. Its cultivation of simple souls and its avoidance of the intellectual side of religion have, among other practical worldly motives, chiefly the aim of concentration on what pays best in terms of membership and, one must add, money.

Self-centredness is not quite the same thing as self-interest. In some sections of the Church it comes nearer to self-worship. Whether more in the one form or in the other this collective attitude on the part of the Church may have much to do with the alienation of the world from religion. If these remarks appear uncharitable, let the critics consider whether there is no church in Christendom which does make this impression and reflect that it is only a difference in degree. It is not healthy for an institution to regard itself as holy. That is the formula for a self-centredness which is the reverse of true spirituality. If it does so regard itself it will invert ends and means and become irrelevant to the civilization which it should serve. If individual Christians should be ready to admit error let the Church breathe that spirit. I cannot help thinking that confession of past errors in points of biblical criticism would do much to lead faith out of addictions into something deeper.*

Let us look at that threatened Fourth Phase as the challenge of the situation to the Church to put an end

* If I may be allowed a suggestion it would be that Anglo-Catholics should study the principles of the Christengemeinschaft, the headquarters of which is in Stuttgart. Its main principle is that worship should not be so much a matter of ideas and feelings as a sustained act of will in following the inward purport of a ritual act through its successive stages toward mystical union with Christ. It is like the Mass, but is not so called, and it is quite the opposite to merely being devout while something wonderful happens outside you. It is of the nature, rather, of a collective spiritual exercise.

to drifting and to make a response more creative than routine. To recover freshness of spirit the Church needs a new Reformation. What ought to be its guiding principles? The first should be a definite break with those of the past. This will involve the express rejection by the Christian conscience of the position maintained in the semi-official Report entitled *Toward the Conversion of England*. A committee, presided over by Bishop Chavasse, had been appointed to make recommendations "with special reference to the spiritual needs and prevailing intellectual outlook of the non-worshipping members of the community". The committee reported that "it is the presentation of the Gospel, not its content, that changes with succeeding generations". This Report must be definitely rejected because it is based on the false assumption that traditional religion, in substance and content, meets the spiritual needs of non-churchgoers. It does not, and the Church ought to have strength of mind enough to recognize that either-or and not postulate that it can have things both ways.

In one sense it can. Christianity can be conceived as a house with two storeys—a ground floor and an upper room. The upper room is the Gospel; the ground floor is some system of principles which is compatible with the Gospel, but does not include it. We might then speak of a greater and a lesser Christianity. But that is not what the Report means. It means something palpably at variance with possibilities. In order to meet the needs of non-churchgoers, the Report devotes itself to things which affect churchgoers only. It insists upon a knowledge of the Bible (one pictures Bishop Chavasse, Bible in hand, calling on Bertrand Russell), but does not apparently mention biblical criticism. (Lord Russell would hardly be so tactless as to raise the point.) When, again, the Report speaks of two stages in evangelism, the first the arousing of interest and then "bringing the convert to the point of decision", one has only to think of a few names in order to realize the silliness of such a reply to the terms of reference. And there is much more in the Report that vulgar children might gibe at, but at least it is optimistic. It tells us that "there are not wanting signs that if the Church would speak with conviction and authority the nation would gladly hearken". In this it is supported by a pamphlet issued by the World's Evangelical Alliance which assures us that "if (young people) hear someone speak with authority, with certainty, and with boldness then they will be ready to listen". The only unfortunate feature in the situation, according to the Report, is "a wholesale drift from organized religion".

I have quoted these passages in order to give a concrete picture of one of the two wrong roads which the Church ought definitely to refuse to follow in its approach to the world beyond its borders. It is the way of conservatism, and these two publications show us what it is like.

Conservatism of at all a rigid kind makes for irreligion in two ways. In the first place, it ignores psychological possibilities, and if preachers bank on what is impossible they promote whatever may be the alternative to it. Psychologically speaking, "modern" means "not open to conversion to old-world lines of thought without some change in its substance and content". This would still be true even if all change meant a change for the worse. There are types of religion which one just cannot belong to because one's mind has got moulded into some other shape. I could not personally revert to the Old Evangelicalism in which I was brought up any more than my hair can revert in colour and quantity to what it was eighty years ago. And I am only half modern, if that. This is no argument against the Old Evangelicalism in itself— I certainly do not imagine that I am a criterion of truth—but it does illustrate the unreality of talking about the conversion of England to creeds which so few can believe.

And, secondly, the greater the insistence upon verbal orthodoxy the greater the inclination of reinterpreters to reply, "Very well, we will swear to every word you wish, but will give it our own new meaning." The phrases of orthodoxy are the starting-point for reductive theology; they cannot crush it.

The other wrong road is the idea that you can convert the world by some sort of liberalism. Convert it to what? Liberalism is not a gospel, a kerugma, the announcement of a wonderful spiritual discovery. It is a reaction against some crudity or irrationality into which it believes orthodoxy to have fallen. Its sphere of action therefore lies within the Church; it is not a message to the world. It starts with the same tradition as conservatism, but instead of cherishing it in its entirety as conservatism does, it proceeds by dropping first one element in it then another until nothing of any emotional value is left. It is that which differentiates religion from humanism that tells, and it is this differentiating factor that liberalism progressively eliminates. Liberals can make some true replies, but these do not amount to showing that faith is still active —much less that it is able to take the field against all unbelief and prevail. Liberalism and conservatism alike show us what the road to a definitely religious national culture cannot possibly be, at any rate until something else has been done. It is almost equally absurd to imagine, with the conservatives, that modern England will flock into churches and mission halls to hear preachers proclaim the theology of a hundred years ago "with authority and conviction and boldness", and, with the liberals, to suppose that it will come if miracles are but treated in a rationalistic way. By and large, liberalism has no kerugma, no wonder-message to the world, to proclaim, and in the absence of one it does not much matter whether it is reasonable or not.*

The third period of modern religion, containing, as it does, within itself survivals of the two earlier phases, is drifting to its end. A mist is creeping over the unseen, but there is no discernible effort to see what is coming and to prepare to meet it—to diagnose before we prescribe. If we ourselves hold archaic views, the youth of England must be eager to hear them. Alternatively, the world does not matter so long as there are some true believers left to share my creed with me. Our present ways will last my time. Or they are what some manual says is Catholic, and that is enough. Is not something like this our attitude, and is it not tragically inadequate in this our day of visitation?

---

* The word "kerugma", a proclamation, is coming into use in theology to emphasize the fact that the Christian faith is not a theory, but an announcement.

Keeroogma is the nearest phonetic rendering. In N.T. times, as also today, the first syllable was pronounced like our "key".

V

THE ALTERNATIVE ROAD

IT was urged at the beginning of this essay that at any given moment of history there is some trend of events in actual process but also the possibility of a higher alternative if the needful moral and spiritual conditions are fulfilled. So it is in the case of the Church today. We see a trend of history following a curve drawn by an ever-increasing pull of science upon the ever-weakening inertia of Christian tradition. That very fact shows us that, for salvation from the end to which the trend is, in spite of all our principles, sweeping us, we must look, not to our principles, but to the potentialities of better things latent in the facts.

The remark was thrown out in passing a little way back (p. 40) that there is one way in which the Church can have it both ways. It can retain its ancient creed for itself and yet possess a fighting philosophy for a counter-attack upon rationalism if it will be content to cut Christianity in half by the recognition of a greater and a lesser Christianity based upon different principles and procedures. Or, to vary the metaphor, if it will look upon the house of faith as having two storeys, a ground floor and an upper room. The ground floor is the general metaphysical world-view inherent in the spirit of religion. The upper room is the traditions and practices of the Christian mystery cult in its various forms.

This view of things is not here put forward primarily as the way of truth or of wise Church policy, but as the significance of the historical situation. Into the soul of the Church there entered, about a hundred years ago, a spirit alien to religion, at least in immediate effect. It came in the service of the sciences and in the name of truth. When the Church accepted it as such— that is to say, for the purposes of science—it thought that a final harmonious synthesis had been reached. This was an illusion, and we now see that events are making for a new temporary balance on the basis of an understanding that religion shall, within the borders of the Church, have the sounds, science the sense—faith to keep its formulas, unbelief to reinter- pret them. All this, of course, is not a transaction be- tween two self-subsistent entities—science and religion —but a description of what is happening in the hearts of Christians, bishops included.

If this is a broadly true analysis of the trend of thought in the Church, what alternative to the drift to disintegration is there open to religion? Surely the only alternative inherent in the facts is for it to organize its forces for a head-on collision with the *proton pseudos* of the enemy—the identification of science with posi- tivism. The case against it is (*a*) that the reduction of religious terms to meanings compatible with postivism does violence to the evidence; (*b*) that religion is veridical of a reality beyond science; (*c*) that even outside the sphere of religion positivism is fallacious; and (*d*) that it is worthier to meditate on the ultimate nature of existence than not to do so.

We will start, then, by considering what sort of thing religion is on its inward side, with the question at the back of our minds whether it can ever be an organ of a truth beyond the scope of science. But the immediate issue is whether religion as an empirical fact is compatible with the re-interpretations of reductive theology. The suggestion here is that religion, in the sense of the mental attitudes expressed in the traditional language of religion, is incompatible with an acceptance of positivism, and that reinterpretations which ignore this fact, falsify their subject-matter.

One definition of religion has already been suggested: religion is the response of man to the Supernatural, in faith that the Supernatural will, in virtue of its utter goodness, respond to him. The general idea and principle of religion is quite simple. It is an asking and taking of help from an unseen source. What the help is for differs in different cases, but all desires and askings must be, as it were, affiliated to the basic desire for a greater, more intrinsic, goodness than one can realize by one's own good resolutions; one must have faith in a spirit of goodness which is really there as a living entity; then, if one truly loves it, keeps it in mind, and tries to conform to it, it, for its part, will respond to you and you will find that you can live on quite another plane of existence than anything that would otherwise have been possible for you. Even when comparatively abstract and impersonal terms are employed, such as the Dharma, the Tao, the Vohu Mano, religion means a willed right relationship between the individual and some cosmic entity with a view to the transformation of the personality in accordance with principles inherent in the spiritual consciousness. As an empirical fact, then, high religion implies a relationship between an individual and an unseen object, and an ideal of life grounded upon that relationship; and efforts to realize that ideal through the mutual approach and response of the Spirit and the believer to one another. And the first inference to be drawn from all this is that all reinterpretations which ignore the principle of right relationship with the unseen are misinterpretations. This does not prove any counter-theory to be true, but it does show that the procedure which has been called Phase Four involves a falsification of the evidence.

Let us remind ourselves once more what precisely it is that we are talking about. It is the significance of the current phase of Church history. It is significant in the extreme because this is the age which is marked by the onset of what will probably prove to be the mortal illness of faith if some quite new remedy is not applied. Extravagant language is most unpleasant, but I ask the reader to judge by his own careful analysis of the evidence whether this remark really is extravagant. The illness in question is a wasting away of the inner substance of religion while its outward forms and activities go on as before. The inner substance of religion is the mentality just described. I have usually spoken of it simply as "religion", but if that word is too ambiguous for the purpose of distinguishing real religion from all the other heterogeneous things also called "religion" let us drop it for a moment and speak of "the mentality aforesaid" instead. For what I have described has been the core and *raison d'être* of Christianity for nineteen centuries as well as of other high religions. The Church's apparatus of doctrines and institutions has existed for the sake of that jewel in the lotus. It is a question of the loss or preservation of something of a distinctive nature which differentiates it from all other human interests.

Let us now change our metaphor and say that religion is hymnody, uttered or unexpressed, together with all those thoughts and attitudes of mind which it may involve. Now why is it that no hymns are being written any more? Hymn-writing by Christians has not been suppressed by a hostile, unbelieving world; something in the hearts of Christians themselves has killed it. It is not anything wicked, wanton, or reprehensible. The wells of praise and thanksgiving have ceased to overflow because that involuntary, subconscious positivism which is the inevitable by-product of science is permeating the Churches. Consider what this means in relation to church services and parochial activities generally. Looked at from short-term points of view, these may really be keeping some sort of religion going, although on an ever-diminishing scale. But when one takes a more comprehensive, long-term view of what is happening, one sees that there is some influence which is eating the mentality aforesaid out of the heart of religion, however orthodox it may strive to be, and that traditional methods of combating it may be contributing to its hold over the thinking of the country.

This is part of what is here meant by the word "trend". A trend of thought which affects the Church is not some line of secularism in the world at large. The trend to naturalism and positivism is something in the cultural atmosphere which is at once cleansing and corrosive, and which undermines faith long before doctrine is consciously affected. Everything in our parishes which goes its own way regardless of the way the world is going will sooner or later become a mask for it.

Now let us dwell for a moment on the thought that the religious spirit may be veridical as the organ of a truth which cannot be rendered exact or scientifically verified, but which has reality-character nevertheless.

Mind is that which apprehends and comprehends. These are two basic urges lying deeper than the psychological processes ordinarily reckoned with. Apprehension is an out-going movement of the soul, comprehension an in-gathering. The words "apprehension" and "comprehension" imply a reference to cognition, but the out-going and the in-gathering urges find expression also in other mental fields. In all of them we find variations of the theme of going forth into the unknown to grasp at something rich and strange and a returning to one's nest of habits and ideas. The going forth of faith in hope to apprehend is especially characteristic of religion. It is the wings of prayer. It is Noah's dove flying forth from its ark in search of a new foothold. If this outgoing of the soul through faith, hope, and love to apprehend its correlative, the Absolute, can be shown to be organic to the fundamental nature of mind it would bring us within sight of an alternative to that process of reduction through reinterpretation which would be equivalent to the death of faith. It would also enable us to understand the ordinary facts of religious life the better. For these two deep undercurrents of the soul manifest themselves only through combination, in very varied measure, with more superficial psychic

D

matter, and especially with group feeling, such as that afforded by membership of a Church. Science is comprehension; even its hypotheses are controlled and limited by it. It represents the mind's homecoming trend.

It has already been pointed out that all types of organized religion—conservative orthodoxy, liberalism, and the rest—all tend to become masks which conceal what is going on beneath the surface. None of these ordinary proceedings therefore can constitute an adequate response to the situation without the addition of other and more novel measures. If, then, a simple continuing of present routine without further reflection or reconsideration is but a drifting with the currents of an unplanned spiritual economy toward the rocks of reductivism and whatever may lie beyond them, what course will a wisely planned spiritual economy steer? Surely it will be that of a dual, instead of a single message and ministry. The Church's kerugma to the world and its ministry to Christian people should each have its own substance and content, its own appropriate methods and institutions. Whether one parish priest can fulfil this dual function or whether something of the nature of interlocked ministries would be required is a question of ecclesiastical organization which does not arise until the principle of a dual ministry has been thought out.

There is here something more than policy. Analysis of the nature of concrete religion points to it. The religion of any at all deeply religious person never starts, as it were, from zero. Taking a certain amount of religious belief for granted it seizes upon some special complex of ideas as something of the highest value or immediate urgency. Any given phase of living religion possesses this dual character of basis and superstructure, of inherited, unquestioned tradition and specialized vision. After a time the vision itself comes to be taken for granted and some new issue supervenes which presupposes it. And so on from age to age, every new religious type as it emerges being able to assume the general validity of a religious standpoint. Now the salient fact about the present situation is that religious beliefs have lost their presuppositions. Christianity rests on an ethical monotheism which is no longer there except as an element in Christianity itself. Its presuppositions being no longer presupposed, the Christian creed now floats in empty space. English tribal tradition is now, or is rapidly becoming, humanist, rationalist, positivist. On top of this there comes, by a sort of geological fault, the religion of the Nicene Creed. It is as though a prefabricated upper room were dumped upon unprepared ground, or as though the soil in which a tree is growing were becoming lost by land-subsidence in the sands of the seashore.

The difficulties caused by the disappearance of the presuppositions of any really vital religion are doubtless largely a consequence of the simple fact of an unplanned spiritual economy, as a result of which colourful details may inhibit attention to ideas likely to seem dry and abstract. But it is probably even more due to the acceptance, sometimes consciously, sometimes instinctively, of the principle of unitary evangelism, as commended, for instance, in the official Report above referred to. This principle not only treats Christianity as a unitary whole; it virtually identifies that whole with its nucleus, "the Gospel". It thus ignores the essential nature of religion, which always, when at all actively present, subsists on two levels, a more generalized and a more specialized. We may speak of these two as basic religion and as the Christian mystery-cult, or as the ground floor and upper room of Christianity.

Let us try, then, to imagine what the content of the preaching of basic religion to the humanist world must be like, reminding ourselves the while that it really must be a matter of preaching and laborious propaganda, and not simply one of book-reading for our own pleasure. There is the task of working to lay ever afresh the moral and spiritual foundations of the life of nations to be done. We must remember too that when it is a question of establishing a higher truth and of laying the foundations of a nobler civilization, educated opinion does count for more than the number of heads. With these reminders not forgotten, we will now set about trying to imagine a really possible line of theological development alternative to that of reductive reinterpretation.

We start with a sense of the intrinsic value of the spiritual consciousness (spoken of above as "the mentality aforesaid") and with an impression of its possibly cognitive, or veridical, character. One aspect of it has already been glanced at—namely, the fact that it involves a sense of relationship with the unseen. This is more than a traditional idea; it is a condition of there being a mode of consciousness of this kind. Another point to note is that the affirmations in which it finds expression are nearly always in the comparative degree. Religion is a pursuit of something higher, deeper, truer than—— Than what? Not "than purely material values", but "than all that human science, art, society, and civilization have to offer". There is a note of world-transcendence in it, so that it suggests the conclusion that man has a dim awareness of the unseen whenever it is not inhibited either by science or by the exigencies of practical life.

Basic religion consists wholly of what is in principle universal; there can be nothing unique in it. Everything unique or specialized belongs to the special mystery cult and implies some further ground of faith over and above man's general spiritual consciousness.

The theology of basic religion will have its polemical side. It will have to show that positivism is fallacious; that supernaturalism can give a better account of the facts than can naturalism, and so forth, entering into many details which cannot be touched on here—I mean criticisms of positivism which have actually been advanced by philosophers, including those of the last century.

It is still more important that Christians should have a metaphysic of the universe which can be imagined and which will provide an intellectual basis for practical religion. This will be called Gnosticism, but let us not be scared by words. Gnosticism of this sort has a deeper rationality than has positivism, for it is always more rational to think than not to think when the object of thought is something so real as the universe or the ultimate ground of existence, even if our thinking ends in wondering and guesswork and not in actual knowledge. The metaphysical imagination is not phantasy; phantasy is what Freud called pleasure-thinking, whereas the metaphysical imagination is a means for trying to grasp the content of pure reason when applied to objects beyond the scope of science.

How then can we best picture the Absolute—the source of all things, itself unconditioned by anything outside itself?

The Absolute is infinitely contentful, determinate, *saguna*, for one thing can proceed from another only in virtue of the attributes of the latter. This is a wider principle than that of causality and does not imply a causal relation between the Absolute and the universe.

The richest, most contentful, mode of existence known to us is that of the human personality. This therefore must provide our main symbol for picturing the Absolute. Personality is consciousness and characterful life, and so we have to think of the Absolute.

The particular character which he must of necessity have is that in virtue of which he is the creator of all things visible and invisible. What keeps a person solitary is his individuality, which tends to turn him into a monad; what overcomes this tendency is love. If God is love it will imply a refusal on his part to be a self-sufficient monad, for the idea of a being who loved infinitely and would be loved involves that of a desire for innumerable non-egos capable of emotional responsiveness, and that of an Absolute which was also love implies a will that they should come into existence. But there is nothing but God and nowhere but God; he can create only by inducing a change within himself, the one self-existent life. A refusal to be Sole-existent would mean a surrender of his unitary selfhood, so that one all-embracing life would be no longer controlled by the central self-consciousness of the Absolute which would thus become an Absolute no longer, but a God and world in relation to one another. The world would be, as it were, one plane, or mode, of the Absolute, in which its divine character had been reduced to latency; life would be life uncontrolled by anything except the conditions of finitude and multiplicity. Each element in universal life would become a loveless little "I am I" unless controlled either by some mechanism of non-egoism, such as that of reproduction or of herd-feeling, or else by the emergence of latent Spirit into empirical reality. Evil would thus be an inevitable product of the "panspermia", or infinite multiplicity and multifariousness of the world-seed. So also are all those creatures which are so weird or horrible in human eyes, but which, a modern prophet assures us, shall all, through innumerable reincarnations, attain at last to a unitive knowledge of Brahma.

A world-view of this kind illuminates the problem of knowledge as well as that of evil. For omnipresent mind, in the sense of a universal mind immanent within all things, and not only in that of a transcendental mind to which all things are presented, is latent aware-ness of all things, and the mechanisms by means of which it takes shape as a particular person's knowledge of particular objects are not the ultimate ground of it.

It fits in, too, with the problem of relationship. Nothing can stand in any sort of relation to anything else except in virtue of some ground of common existence and relationship which is metaphysically prior to them both, and which is itself unitary. Similarly with regard to the problems of omnipotence and the moral order. How often one hears it said, "It seems so strange that such a good person as So-and-So should have had to suffer so much. I can't understand it." The implied idea here is that of a God acting within the world under conditions of time and space, just as a managing director acts within the same system of things as what he manages. That would be for God to make himself a creature among all other creatures, but one charged, in virtue of his possession of omnipotence, with the special duty of seeing to it that everything in the universe happened as it ought to happen. But if God can create only by bringing about a change within himself whereby his knowledge and power relatively to the details of creation are reduced to latency and subject to the conditions of slow re-emergence in innumerably varied finite forms, the case is different. Omnipotence is God's power to create a universe—not a power to act as a magician within it. It should, in fact, be a definite principle that the ideas by which a general religious world-view is described should not be derived from the relations of a person to other persons or things. The primary ideas of a spiritual philosophy should be such as will be suited to persons inclined to naturalism, and for such persons anthropomorphic imagery is a provocation. The idea that "All are but parts of one stupendous whole whose body nature is, and God the soul" might have been useful if it had not been linked with a moral indifferentism that is offensive to Christian feeling. It is not the conception of the organic unity of God and the universe that is so open to objection, but the suggestion that God is as fully and perfectly revealed in inanimate objects or in some vile scoundrel as in angelic hearts. That does not by any means necessarily follow from a theology of organism.

I have felt obliged to dwell on this line of thought at some length in order to show that an alternative to present theological tendencies is a real possibility. It is, moreover, a course which would enable the Church to fulfil her duty to the humanist world almost for the first time, and so has its practical as well as its intellectual aspect. Its guiding idea is that of checking the drift from Phase Three to Phase Four and restoring the intellectual presuppositions of religion by means of a spiritualist philosophy and some sort of parochial organization to promote it. As part of it, social ethics should not be forgotten. The one thing that would most surely wreck the plan would be any resort to unitary evangelism. The ordinary church services could go on exactly as usual. All that I have urged is that the New Testament and everything founded on it should be excluded from "ground-floor" activities.

These proposals have reference to the present position of the Christian faith in this country and we ought to make an effort to envisage it. It is grave in the extreme. The great difficulty is epistemological. By what process can we possibly become aware of such facts as those belief in which has always constituted the very heart of the Christian faith? How can we know anything about particular transcendental acts of God or of a pre-existent Christ as are implied in the ideas of incarnation or atonement or any other divine actions in time and place? The traditional answer has always been "By faith in revealed truth". But people have faith in all sorts of mistaken ideas; how are we to know that faith is justified in our own case, but not in that of people who hold beliefs different from ours?

The religious world is full of alleged revelations. How are we to distinguish real revelations from delusions? We should like to believe, but how can we know that we are not kidding ourselves? If there is such a thing as a brief summary of the essence of Christianity, it is that lovely passage in the second chapter of Philippians, but how are such transcendental events apprehensible at all? I do not say comprehensible, but by what trustworthy process can we get the idea of it into our minds? And that is not the whole difficulty. Having got it, we find that this idea of a saviour and revealer of divine truth is closely akin to much that we find in the Gnostic and Hermetic literature of the age. Very broadly speaking, we may say that St. Paul is akin to Gnosticism, St. John to Philo's philosophy, and Hebrews to Judaism and to the sacrificial ideas of the whole heathen world. By what valid process of thought can we say that these Gnostic, Jewish, speculative, and pagan ideas constitute a divine revelation when applied to Christ, but not in their other connections? And yet further; the Christian story not only resembles mythological ideas, it contains them. Is Gabriel a real or a mythological figure? If you eliminate him, what you have left is a story that a Jewish girl had a phantasy that she was going to be the mother of the Messiah. That will not do. Mythical or not, Gabriel is essential.

I need not, surely, further stress the point that the outstanding feature of the present phase of religious thought is an enormously enhanced realization within the Christian Church of the epistemological difficulties of its creed. Until this is seen we cannot understand the significance of the various schools of modern theology. They are not gratuitous speculations; they are reactions to a situation.

I hope that the relevance of the distinction between ground-floor theology and the theology of the upper room, between religion in general and any given mystery cult, is now clearer. I have tried to show that it is quite possible to build a theology on the specific nature of the spiritual consciousness independently of any specialized faith. The procedure and underlying mental attitude of these two lines of religious thought are quite different, and each seems to be free from the weaknesses which beset the other, so that the idea naturally suggests itself that perhaps they are mutually complementary. Be that as it may, the immediate point is that the difficulties of the specialized creeds of Christendom seem to show that more attention should be devoted to general principles. It is the specialized creeds which are drifting into Phase Four.

Let us imagine traditional Christianity with, as it were, inverted stress. It would present a type which was different from any of the four phases which represent the natural course of modern history. In the first place, there would be an inversion of functional emphasis. A church is not only a special interest with its own traditions, its own membership, apart from the general life of the country. It is also an institution for the spiritualization of English civilization. It has both its ecclesiastical, or devotional, and its national, or cultural, aspect. Viewed from this latter standpoint, its main function is to convince at least fifty-one per cent. of the more reflective portion of the population that a spiritualist philosophy rationally holds good. It is not simply a matter of numbers. For the finding of truth and the fashioning of a national culture those who can appreciate critical points of history and metaphysics represent the key position to be won, and the way religion is presented should correspond with the natural approach to it for thoughtful, educated people. Religion approached from a distance displays a perspective and proportion different from what it looks like inside the Church, and the first borderline territory which humanists have to cross in order to reach a genuinely religious position is metaphysical and cosmological. They must have a general conception of the universe that can make religion broadly rational.

When a broadly religious position has been reached it will usually be felt that bare theism is rather bloodless and contentless. Either the new believer will be likely to lapse into humanism again or he will need a church with a specialized creed which he can join. By supposition, he is acutely conscious of the unknowableness or the obsoleteness or the legendary character of much that is contained in our present creeds and so a reversion to literalism is out of the question. It does not enter into the choice before modern man. But the objections to many Christian doctrines hold good only if they are presented as quite literal facts and their acceptance as a rule of faith for all good churchfolk, and they need not be so presented. As a world of wonderings, hopes, hypotheses, possibilities, and free individual convictions a loved and revered tradition is in most cases essential to vital religion. The spiritual consciousness needs a mystery cult to bring it into life and it takes its moral and emotional quality from it. The Christian saga is the most beautiful and the most redemptive world of ideas there ever has been or ever will be. It is as though a man's soul had slept until the kiss of a divine Redeemer awakened it—a mystic happening that must be renewed generation after generation.

The great problem, then, is how to keep our myths —not how to get rid of them. And they differ so much in character among themselves that we should avoid all procedure by rule of thumb with one common treatment for them all. For some we may take the line that we cannot know that what is unknowable is untrue. We cannot know, for instance, that the incarnation of a pre-existent Christ in fulfilment of a mission of salvation is a cosmological impossibility; it is merely unknowable, and one may legitimately hold to the thought that either it is true or that his relation to man's spiritual well-being is such that it is "as if" it were true. Consider again how much might be made of a treatment of the idea of a resurrection of the body on lines different from those alike of literalism, of reduction, and of mere metaphor. It is the orthodox who are allowing valuable doctrines to fall into disuse, such as those of the Second Coming, the Atonement, or the Logos—doctrines which are formally declared to be immutable and essential and then shelved in favour of light-weight religion.

Quite the most striking example of this virtual throwing away of invaluable doctrines rather than abandon a crude literalism is seen in the handling of the Easter story in nearly all parishes. The circumstances are that civilization is fast losing its belief in a life after death and there are grounds for suspecting that some of the clergy are beginning to feel in the same way, with careful concealment at the same time

of their inmost thoughts. The point of Church tradition with which this tendency comes into most direct
conflict is the very one on which the Church was
founded—namely, the Resurrection. Here, for once,
the Church would find itself in an extremely strong
position if only it had the generalship and the long
view to take advantage of it. The overwhelming
weight of evidence points to the conclusion that Christ
did manifest himself from the world beyond death to
certain people, one of whom had regarded him as
mad and another who was a fierce enemy. When one
considers the first-rate character of I Cor. xv. 3-8 as
historical evidence, together with the strength of
certain lines of further corroboration, one sees what a
remarkable opportunity there is for the Church to
change its front without abandoning its faith. I have
not forgotten that it is not my task to expound doctrines or to pursue critical studies except in so far as is
necessary in order to make the present situation as
clear as possible, but that need for clearness does
demand a little more critical comment.

The cardinal issue between Christianity and naturalism is that of survival; the Church has always
based its belief in this on the Resurrection; it has
taken its idea of the Resurrection from the Gospel
stories of it; these have become valueless for any other
pupose than that of Easter festivals; as a serious basis
of faith they are a downright provocation. But if we
look a little closely at them, we discover something
highly significant about them. They are not glorifica-
tion legends, as the Birth narratives so plainly are.
They are not of a type that mere imagination and
emotion would run to. Nor are they of the impossibly

unnatural kind suggested by Professor Bultmann and his friends. The only one which has a literary, fictional look about it is the story of the walk to Emmaus, and that is clearly of a secondary character which pre-supposes the idea of the Resurrection. The others are all attempts to get over a difficulty. They might be called refutation legends, counter-theory legends, or controversial legends. We are told that "some doubted"—doubted, that is to say, whether the Appearances were of anything more than an unsub-stantial shade from Sheol. The Jews had the idea of a shadowy existence in the nether world. They had also the idea of a resuscitation of dead bodies which was to be the explanation of Christ's reappearances. The doubters were the Sheolists; devotional feeling demanded some-thing more solid and substantial. Hence the stories. If the risen Christ could pass through closed doors, there was no need for the stone to be rolled away, but the tomb had to be seen empty. So too the clasping of Christ's feet by the women, the story of St. Thomas, the "Touch me not" to Mary Magdalene, the fish-eating story, and the words "Handle me and see, for a spirit hath not flesh and bones as ye see me have", all point to the conclusion that the Appearances were rather ghostlike. Otherwise there would have been no need for so much protestation.

To summarize, then. A certain curve of history has led from the deep faith of the last century to a point at which there is a tendency for the whole content of religious thought to become secularized and cease to be genuinely religious any longer. This is happening partly as the result of a perfectly straightforward interest in psychology, partly owing to the increasing use of deceptive language and the concealment of a preacher's real thoughts. As a means for stemming this tendency, a policy of conservatism is self-defeating. The soul goes out of words and they become a shell beneath which spiritual disintegration goes on unnoticed.

The gravest element in the situation is the threatened reign of pulpit dishonesty. It will be due to the extreme discrepancy between traditional orthodoxy and modern tendency; to the doctrine of simple souls; to the oath of assent; to the short-term, managerial point of view; to the principle of reinterpretation; to the inertia of routine; to the lack of a sense of the significance of things happening and of words written. Our principles are so admirable, our application of them so elusive. Consider, for instance, the principle that in all discussions of the apparently miraculous honesty begins with the honest handling of the historical evidence, whether it be evidence for or evidence against. "We must believe neither without evidence nor against evidence", says a distinguished theologian. And yet only four or five pages earlier he had been arguing for the credibility of a miracle which has the actual, critically sifted, evidence overwhelmingly against it. He argues for it on the ground that one can never know "that God never bends physical fact into special conformity with divine intention"— without so much as one word of reference to any evidence. If the Church is to make a successful stand against the tongue-in-cheek theology of reinterpreters (I am not referring to any Lutherans), it must be much franker than this, especially in its parochial practice.

It is possible that naturalism may ultimately prove itself true, but it has not done so yet; life is mostly a matter of banking on uncertainties, and Christians are people who bank on the Supernatural, on God, on the high purposiveness of existence, on a Hereafter. It is as though we said, "Ich hab meine Sache auf Gott gestellt." But we must recognize that it is only in the presence of real uncertainties that faith based on existential attitudes is legitimate and that sincerity comes first.

Up to this point, in tracing the course of religious thought and conduct within the Church of England since the time when, nearly a hundred years ago, it began to open the door of the house of faith to let science come inside, we have taken no account of any motives except the religious, the intellectual, and the parochial. These did determine history. It has been a story, not of events, but of spiritual change. In the main its course has been the resultant of two spiritual forces, but in recent times a commercial factor is coming to exercise an increasing influence. The publication of religious literature is more dependent upon trade conditions than formerly. When people feel that some aspect of truth is being overlooked the normal reaction is to write books or articles about it and hope for publication. I am not speaking of those who write for any other reason than because they have been quite disinterestedly moved so to do. As a general rule they are likely to represent that alternative possibility which in every age tends to pass into a might-have-been. The difficulty is that, to be honest, they must say things likely to arouse the disapproval, first of one side in any controversial matter and then of the other,

E

and so will have no assured body of readers. No publisher will then gamble on the off-chance of their books proving a profitable investment. Down to comparatively recent times the publication of a book written from a more or less detached point of view was not an economic impossibility; perhaps it is becoming so. Whether it be for this reason or because we are not very sure about our own beliefs there seem to be a good many evasive silences in many books written in the religious interest. It is not a healthy symptom. Let our motto be that of the prophet who said: "That which the Lord saith unto me that will I speak. I cannot go beyond the word of the Lord to say either less or more."

There are other lines of thought which are relevant to the religious situation, such as Professor H. H. Price's plea that it is not simply a matter of ideas, but of the need for a deepening of consciousness, for which purpose a practical use might be made of the philosophies of the East. This subject does not come within the scope of a brief outline of thought and practice in the Church of England during the last hundred years. But it has a considerable bearing upon our plans for the present day viewed in relation to future possibilities. For nearly all the mystics of past ages and all creeds have started from some traditional mystery cult. There is no transition from logic to vision; we need a creed as mythological and imaginable as truth will permit. As a preliminary thereto we shall do well to consider the possibility of a third alternative to the choice between conservative tradition and reductive reinterpretation. That alternative would be, surely, an attempt to re-feel and re-state the traditional doctrines of the Church in complete freedom to reject or recast as truth may seem to demand, yet always within the limits laid down by the specific nature of the spiritual consciousness, with its fundamental desire for harmonious relationship with the supernatural and unseen.

The central moral problem for church life which has been precipitated by the coming of demythology is that of insincere belief, and the Church should consider what it is prepared to sacrifice in order to maintain its intellectual integrity. Insincerity, tacit unbelief, tricky reinterpretations, and the like are the nemesis of the old orthodoxy which proclaimed a creed as absolute and necessary truth to be enforced by oaths, execrations, excommunications and even executions. The opposite principle is that of freedom. Priest and people are now recognized as free to believe, doubt, or disbelieve, but on the general understanding that all are hoping to find a truth beyond naturalism, beyond all exercise of the critical reason, beyond poetry. The religious attitude is one that seeks to believe as much as it truthfully can. One may actually believe but little, but the eyes of the soul will be looking toward a dawning of something fuller and clearer. The creeds, in spite of all mistaken beliefs contained in them, symbolize that dawning vision and express it in varying measure according to our personal judgement.

The natural starting-point for modern man when thinking out the problems of religion is naturalism; then comes an appreciation of the moral and social value of religion; then a sense of the beauty of true saintliness and a hope that somehow the possibility of it may be preserved; then a discrimination between the spirit of true religion and the various alloys—some of them very good—which tend to be associated with it; then a tentative trying out of a philosophy of Spirit which would validate faith on the intellectual plane; then a recognition of the great extent to which all this is dependent upon the apparently mythological element in religion. All this is only preliminary to the question what we ought to do about that apparently mythological factor in all vital faith, but a right approach is half-way to a right solution.

APPENDIX

TO solve the problem of attracting people to church there ought to be much more systematic planning than is at present common. To say, as it were, "Here is the service; we will brighten it up for you a bit; now come along" is much too rough and ready. To begin with there should be concern for the purity of our own motives. A parish priest's first aim should not be to fill his church; as primary aim that is a worldly-minded objective. First comes the Church's obligation to fulfil its duty to every class of the population. To that end parishioners everywhere should be thought of as representing various mental types and each type should be separately planned for. Let us consider some of these types.

First come those who are already deeply religious. The only thing I have to say in connection with these is to remark how seldom one hears a devotional sermon. Neither God nor Jesus Christ often comes into a sermon with more than a passing reference.

Secondly come those who can be approached only by worker-priests or worker lay readers, and so far as I am aware, there are none.

Thirdly, there are those who will come to church so long as they feel that they are cheered up by the service and perhaps given a helpful thought or two. But the sermon must be short and the service must go with a swing. Religion must not be too religious if this type of mind is to be attracted to church. Neither moral demands nor those of faith must be pressed too far and neither spoken thought nor readings must be dry. Since it is this type of mind that the Church makes the greatest effort to win there seems to be a danger that organized religion will come to represent a much lower moral level than that of the higher secular interests, to say nothing of its intellectual level.

Finally, there is that class of mind with which this study is chiefly concerned, namely that of those people whose habits of thought and feeling are characteristic of the present time, who tend to non-churchgoing and to humanism, but who might attend services if they found the serious interests of the age well dealt with in them and a distinctively religious outlook ably presented. We will try to imagine what sort of service would best correspond with their needs, whether such a service be possible or not. It is not as a practical proposal but as a speculative analysis of the possibilities of a genuinely religious responsiveness on the part of typically modern minds that we are thinking of it. The following may serve as a first draft for subsequent modification:

Exhortation

Brethren, let us seek to bring our minds into harmony with the faith and hopes of Christian men throughout the ages. Of that faith and of those hopes the creeds remain the symbols. Let every man interpret them as seems to him the truth, remembering that they tell of things beyond the strictness of knowledge. They are indeed tokens of man's apprehension of God, not by exact opinion but by a going forth of the heart. Therefore in freedom and submission, as before the Known and the Unknown, according as every man has received understanding, let us recite the creed of the Church.

The Nicene Creed.

The Collect for the seventh Sunday after Trinity, address perhaps modified.

The Sermon. (In the form of a lecture of, let us say, forty minutes.)

The aim of the rest of the service would be so to "change and deepen consciousness" while it is in progress that some modification of it will remain after it is over. Anything popular in style, anything that goes with a swing, anything superficially attractive, should be avoided; such things would render any touch of mystical consciousness impossible One is tempted to make further suggestions but it would be too much like advertising one's personal tastes.

When one realizes the extreme difficulty of designing a service that could possibly awaken a spirit of worship in late-twentieth-century minds, or of putting things in such a way that they would seem rational without being reductive; when one feels how those concepts and desires of which religion has always been made—such as those of forgiveness or union with God —are becoming unsubstantial, one wonders how many people, by the end of the century, will still possess any capacity for real religion unless, in the meanwhile, some revolutionary change takes place in our philosophy and some radical reorientation in the mind of religion itself.

SOME SUGGESTIONS

1. A COPEC Conference should be held once a quarter, one whole day, probably a Saturday, being devoted to points of social ethics and kindred subjects, priority of speaking and management being given to resident parishioners in preference to members of the congregation coming from other parishes. Such an institution would require a new direction of interest and studies on the part of the parish priest, and this new attitude on his part to the subject would be a reorientation of his outlook. That would, indeed, be the practical argument against the proposal. It is not so much that anything of the kind would necessarily be impracticable. The organizing secretary would be a layman; some keen person, perhaps an undergraduate, might in many cases be found. But there would be a threat to the routine in which vicar and church officers felt comfortable and at home. Things might be said that would upset someone. But all this means that the mind of the Church is not rightly adjusted to its task; it needs reorientation, metanoia, rebirth.

2. A second proposal might be this: Let the service on the morning of the second Sunday in the month be primarily for the benefit of non-Christians and persons interested in the intellectual aspect of religion and let the fact be advertised throughout the parish. The sermons should not be devoted to Christian apologetics, but to what I have called "the ground floor of religion". There are normally a hundred and four

Sunday sermons a year preached in a church. If twelve of these were addressed to persons in intellectual need it would still leave ninety-two for the faithful. Why does one never hear of anything of the kind being done? Surely for the same reason as before: apart from quite exceptional cases the Church is not mentally adapted to its tasks in the modern world. I do not mean the expression derisively, but surely the attractions of a happy congregational tea-party type of religion are partly responsible for the Church's neglect of its strayed sheep.

3. Even on other Sunday mornings the sermon should last at least half an hour and should be concerned with some definite idea or principle. No lecturer can adequately handle a serious subject in shorter time. Two hymns are quite enough. Descriptive Bible scenes and character studies, anecdotal matter, and other comparatively light programme should be reserved for evensong. A short-term congregational opportunism is preventing the Church even from envisaging its major tasks.

4. I suggest the occasional use of some such exhortation as the following at the commencement of a service: "Friends and seekers after God, we are about to engage in solemn worship after the manner of our fathers. Worshippers must exercise their own judgement as to what is, in all probability, legendary in the Bible readings, what substantially historical. But the two are inseparably interwoven and legend may be a channel of spiritual truth. Regard the creeds as symbols of the continuity of the faith rather than as summaries of exact information. If any worshipper should feel distressed by anything in the service or in

the sermon or by any other matter bearing upon his faith or peace of heart let him tell me and the matter will be considered."

5. We will now think of a few reforms at a higher than parochial level. Let us imagine an arrangement whereby parishes were combined two and two. The vicar of one of each pair of parishes and the curate of the other would minister to the two congregations as at present. The second incumbent, not necessarily in holy orders, assisted by a voluntary staff, would have no duties inside the church except for one monthly sermon. The rest of his time would be taken up with visiting with a view to serious discussions, chiefly with non-Christians. He would have the use of both parish halls where he could lecture on any subject bearing upon a religious world-view. He could organize conferences as he thought fit. There would thus be two orders of priests, the pastors and the scholastics. Before induction into a scholastic living the new incumbent should be required to pass a fresh examination at some university. It would be quite possible for a diocese voluntarily to organize itself in a way that would approximate to some such scheme. The Church does amalgamate parishes for practical reasons, but when it comes to the harder tasks of its service of humanity it cannot see the path for lions.

6. Why should not the Church Congress—a sort of theological counterpart to the British Association—be revived?

7. Another possible reform would be that of the syllabus for theological examinations. There is so much study necessary for a right understanding of the

modern situation that room should be made for it by drastic excisions of obsolescent matter. The whole of Church history and doctrine between the years A.D. 200 and 1800 should be reserved for specialists. It should not enter into the training of the parochial clergy. Theology is not an end in itself and creeds are not ends in themselves; they are means to the spiritual welfare of man, and what that welfare requires varies from age to age. Attention devoted to old-world controversies must inevitably render the minds of the clergy ill-adapted to the tasks of the modern world.

8. I have been assured by a highly expert teacher that the Agreed Syllabus of Religious Instruction in schools is most unsatisfactory, (a) in that many passages are included which produce results the opposite of that intended, and (b) in that the Syllabus gives little or no guidance for the teacher in such cases. My friend quoted cases. If half a dozen or a dozen schoolmasters and mistresses would institute a private cooperative inquiry into the matter and publish their findings valuable conclusions might be reached. Any official action subsequently taken would then be far wiser than it would have been had no such expert private action preceded it. A choice between a more modernist and a more conservative syllabus would be one possibility.

9. Another measure might be a partial reorganization of parochial life on the basis of things as they actually are. In actual fact the Church of England is a body with a nucleus of believers and a large fringe of adherents, many of them creedless and even atheists. The actual reason why these unbelievers are well-wishers of the Church is usually that they think it is a

valuable social institution. It is far from being all that it might be, they probably feel, but it is valuable nevertheless. (Section 3.) Not even the most extreme Anglo-Catholics object to the existence of this fringe; they are only concerned for the preservation of the conditions of sacramental life for the believers, as they understand those conditions to be. Why then continue to pretend that the Church of England is essentially a body of people unanimously devoted to the Apostles' Creed? It is unreal, just as the pretence of assenting to the Thirty-nine Articles is unreal. Why should there not be a formal admission of the fact that there are two degrees of church-membership, together constituting, as it were, an outer and an inner church? If every parishioner were asked whether he wished to be enrolled as an associate member of the Church of England, no credal confession necessary and no obligations being incurred, there would then be two parochial rolls, the communicants' and the residential. The result, with an incumbent at all alive to his opportunities, might be a much closer contact between Church and parish. There might, for instance, be two tribunes, or howsoever else called, appointed by the incumbent every year to be in charge of the interests of those on the residential roll, which it would be their duty to keep up to date, one tribune being a man, the other a woman, and preferably friendly agnostics.

10. Yet one more dreamland proposal. It is the one which I would most gladly have avoided because it is so hard to talk about it without an appearance of cantankerousness, and all the more so since it refers to a point owing to which I have not been able to hold

any regular position in the ministry for over forty years. Surely the requirement of an oath of assent to the Thirty-nine Articles is open to the very strongest objection both on moral and on more specifically religious grounds. I refer both to the general principle of the oath as a test and also to the equivocations inevitably involved. It serves no good purpose, being relevant only to the political plots and religious factions of past centuries. In a correspondence in *The Times* on one aspect of the subject in July, 1956, one or two correspondents declared that candidates for ordination had no objection to the oath and its implications. That means that the test is operating as a ground of selection; those who do object do not offer themselves as ordination candidates. Does the Church expressly desire this restriction? It is much to be hoped that, before so very long, some bishop will announce that he intends personally to satisfy himself of the thorough fitness of every ordinand for the ministry and, on finding him fit, to ordain him without insisting upon subscription, should the candidate have any scruples in the matter. It would then rest with the State to decide whether or not it should take action to prevent the bishop from carrying out his intention.

As an example of what the clergy are required to assent to on oath we may take the following: "Christ did truly rise again from death and took again his body with flesh, bones, and all things appertaining to the perfection of Man's nature; wherewith he ascended into Heaven, and there sitteth until he return to judge all Men at the last day." And the accompanying Declaration explains that "no man . . . shall . . . put his own sense or comment to be the meaning of the Article, but shall take it in the literal and grammatical sense". The legal aspect of the case is not the point, nor is even the equivocal nature of the subscription the chief trouble. It is the false oath.